FREE Test Taking Tips DVD Offer

To help us better serve you, we have developed a Test Taking Tips DVD that we would like to give you for FREE. **This DVD covers world-class test taking tips that you can use to be even more successful when you are taking your test.**

All that we ask is that you email us your feedback about your study guide. Please let us know what you thought about it – whether that is good, bad or indifferent.

To get your **FREE Test Taking Tips DVD**, email freedvd@studyguideteam.com with "FREE DVD" in the subject line and the following information in the body of the email:

    a. The title of your study guide.

    b. Your product rating on a scale of 1-5, with 5 being the highest rating.

    c. Your feedback about the study guide. What did you think of it?

    d. Your full name and shipping address to send your free DVD.

If you have any questions or concerns, please don't hesitate to contact us at freedvd@studyguideteam.com.

Thanks again!

NNAT Grade 2 Study Guide

Gifted and Talented Test Preparation with Practice Exam Questions for the Naglieri Nonverbal Ability Test Grade 2 [3rd Edition]

TPB Publishing

Written and edited by Test Prep Books.

Interested in buying more than 10 copies of our product? Contact us about bulk discounts:
bulkorders@studyguideteam.com

ISBN 13: 9781628458923
ISBN 10: 1628458925

Table of Contents

Quick Overview

As you draw closer to taking your exam, effective preparation becomes more and more important. Thankfully, you have this study guide to help you get ready. Use this guide to help keep your studying on track and refer to it often.

This study guide contains several key sections that will help you be successful on your exam. The guide contains tips for what you should do the night before and the day of the test. Also included are test-taking tips. Knowing the right information is not always enough. Many well-prepared test takers struggle with exams. These tips will help equip you to accurately read, assess, and answer test questions.

A large part of the guide is devoted to showing you what content to expect on the exam and to helping you better understand that content. In this guide are practice test questions so that you can see how well you have grasped the content. Then, answer explanations are provided so that you can understand why you missed certain questions.

Don't try to cram the night before you take your exam. This is not a wise strategy for a few reasons. First, your retention of the information will be low. Your time would be better used by reviewing information you already know rather than trying to learn a lot of new information. Second, you will likely become stressed as you try to gain a large amount of knowledge in a short amount of time. Third, you will be depriving yourself of sleep. So be sure to go to bed at a reasonable time the night before. Being well-rested helps you focus and remain calm.

Be sure to eat a substantial breakfast the morning of the exam. If you are taking the exam in the afternoon, be sure to have a good lunch as well. Being hungry is distracting and can make it difficult to focus. You have hopefully spent lots of time preparing for the exam. Don't let an empty stomach get in the way of success!

When travelling to the testing center, leave earlier than needed. That way, you have a buffer in case you experience any delays. This will help you remain calm and will keep you from missing your appointment time at the testing center.

Be sure to pace yourself during the exam. Don't try to rush through the exam. There is no need to risk performing poorly on the exam just so you can leave the testing center early. Allow yourself to use all of the allotted time if needed.

Remain positive while taking the exam even if you feel like you are performing poorly. Thinking about the content you should have mastered will not help you perform better on the exam.

Once the exam is complete, take some time to relax. Even if you feel that you need to take the exam again, you will be well served by some down time before you begin studying again. It's often easier to convince yourself to study if you know that it will come with a reward!

Test-Taking Strategies

1. Predicting the Answer

When you feel confident in your preparation for a multiple-choice test, try predicting the answer before reading the answer choices. This is especially useful on questions that test objective factual knowledge. By predicting the answer before reading the available choices, you eliminate the possibility that you will be distracted or led astray by an incorrect answer choice. You will feel more confident in your selection if you read the question, predict the answer, and then find your prediction among the answer choices. After using this strategy, be sure to still read all of the answer choices carefully and completely. If you feel unprepared, you should not attempt to predict the answers. This would be a waste of time and an opportunity for your mind to wander in the wrong direction.

2. Reading the Whole Question

Too often, test takers scan a multiple-choice question, recognize a few familiar words, and immediately jump to the answer choices. Test authors are aware of this common impatience, and they will sometimes prey upon it. For instance, a test author might subtly turn the question into a negative, or he or she might redirect the focus of the question right at the end. The only way to avoid falling into these traps is to read the entirety of the question carefully before reading the answer choices.

3. Looking for Wrong Answers

Long and complicated multiple-choice questions can be intimidating. One way to simplify a difficult multiple-choice question is to eliminate all of the answer choices that are clearly wrong. In most sets of answers, there will be at least one selection that can be dismissed right away. If the test is administered on paper, the test taker could draw a line through it to indicate that it may be ignored; otherwise, the test taker will have to perform this operation mentally or on scratch paper. In either case, once the obviously incorrect answers have been eliminated, the remaining choices may be considered. Sometimes identifying the clearly wrong answers will give the test taker some information about the correct answer. For instance, if one of the remaining answer choices is a direct opposite of one of the eliminated answer choices, it may well be the correct answer. The opposite of obviously wrong is obviously right! Of course, this is not always the case. Some answers are obviously incorrect simply because they are irrelevant to the question being asked. Still, identifying and eliminating some incorrect answer choices is a good way to simplify a multiple-choice question.

4. Don't Overanalyze

Anxious test takers often overanalyze questions. When you are nervous, your brain will often run wild, causing you to make associations and discover clues that don't actually exist. If you feel that this may be a problem for you, do whatever you can to slow down during the test. Try taking a deep breath or counting to ten. As you read and consider the question, restrict yourself to the particular words used by the author. Avoid thought tangents about what the author *really* meant, or what he or she was *trying* to say. The only things that matter on a multiple-choice test are the words that are actually in the question. You must avoid reading too much into a multiple-choice question, or supposing that the writer meant something other than what he or she wrote.

5. No Need for Panic

It is wise to learn as many strategies as possible before taking a multiple-choice test, but it is likely that you will come across a few questions for which you simply don't know the answer. In this situation, avoid panicking. Because most multiple-choice tests include dozens of questions, the relative value of a single wrong answer is small. As much as possible, you should compartmentalize each question on a multiple-choice test. In other words, you should not allow your feelings about one question to affect your success on the others. When you find a question that you either don't understand or don't know how to answer, just take a deep breath and do your best. Read the entire question slowly and carefully. Try rephrasing the question a couple of different ways. Then, read all of the answer choices carefully. After eliminating obviously wrong answers, make a selection and move on to the next question.

6. Confusing Answer Choices

When working on a difficult multiple-choice question, there may be a tendency to focus on the answer choices that are the easiest to understand. Many people, whether consciously or not, gravitate to the answer choices that require the least concentration, knowledge, and memory. This is a mistake. When you come across an answer choice that is confusing, you should give it extra attention. A question might be confusing because you do not know the subject matter to which it refers. If this is the case, don't eliminate the answer before you have affirmatively settled on another. When you come across an answer choice of this type, set it aside as you look at the remaining choices. If you can confidently assert that one of the other choices is correct, you can leave the confusing answer aside. Otherwise, you will need to take a moment to try to better understand the confusing answer choice. Rephrasing is one way to tease out the sense of a confusing answer choice.

7. Your First Instinct

Many people struggle with multiple-choice tests because they overthink the questions. If you have studied sufficiently for the test, you should be prepared to trust your first instinct once you have carefully and completely read the question and all of the answer choices. There is a great deal of research suggesting that the mind can come to the correct conclusion very quickly once it has obtained all of the relevant information. At times, it may seem to you as if your intuition is working faster even than your reasoning mind. This may in fact be true. The knowledge you obtain while studying may be retrieved from your subconscious before you have a chance to work out the associations that support it. Verify your instinct by working out the reasons that it should be trusted.

8. Key Words

Many test takers struggle with multiple-choice questions because they have poor reading comprehension skills. Quickly reading and understanding a multiple-choice question requires a mixture of skill and experience. To help with this, try jotting down a few key words and phrases on a piece of scrap paper. Doing this concentrates the process of reading and forces the mind to weigh the relative importance of the question's parts. In selecting words and phrases to write down, the test taker thinks about the question more deeply and carefully. This is especially true for multiple-choice questions that are preceded by a long prompt.

9. Subtle Negatives

One of the oldest tricks in the multiple-choice test writer's book is to subtly reverse the meaning of a question with a word like *not* or *except*. If you are not paying attention to each word in the question, you can easily be led astray by this trick. For instance, a common question format is, "Which of the following is...?" Obviously, if the question instead is, "Which of the following is not...?," then the answer will be quite different. Even worse, the test makers are aware of the potential for this mistake and will include one answer choice that would be correct if the question were not negated or reversed. A test taker who misses the reversal will find what he or she believes to be a correct answer and will be so confident that he or she will fail to reread the question and discover the original error. The only way to avoid this is to practice a wide variety of multiple-choice questions and to pay close attention to each and every word.

10. No Patterns

One of the more dangerous ideas that circulates about multiple-choice tests is that the correct answers tend to fall into patterns. These erroneous ideas range from a belief that B and C are the most common right answers, to the idea that an unprepared test-taker should answer "A-B-A-C-A-D-A-B-A." It cannot be emphasized enough that pattern-seeking of this type is exactly the WRONG way to approach a multiple-choice test. To begin with, it is highly unlikely that the test maker will plot the correct answers according to some predetermined pattern. The questions are scrambled and delivered in a random order. Furthermore, even if the test maker was following a pattern in the assignation of correct answers, there is no reason why the test taker would know which pattern he or she was using. Any attempt to discern a pattern in the answer choices is a waste of time and a distraction from the real work of taking the test. A test taker would be much better served by extra preparation before the test than by reliance on a pattern in the answers.

FREE DVD OFFER

Don't forget that doing well on your exam includes both understanding the test content and understanding how to use what you know to do well on the test. We offer a completely FREE Test Taking Tips DVD that covers world class test taking tips that you can use to be even more successful when you are taking your test.

All that we ask is that you email us your feedback about your study guide. To get your **FREE Test Taking Tips DVD**, email freedvd@studyguideteam.com with "FREE DVD" in the subject line and the following information in the body of the email:

- The title of your study guide.
- Your product rating on a scale of 1-5, with 5 being the highest rating.
- Your feedback about the study guide. What did you think of it?
- Your full name and shipping address to send your free DVD.

Introduction to the NNAT3 Level C

Function of the Test

The Naglieri Nonverbal Ability Test (NNAT) is used to measure giftedness in children aged 5 to 17. The NNAT was created by Jack Naglieri, a scientist and Professor of Research and Psychology, and subsequently published by Pearson Education in 2004. The NNAT was created to test nonverbal ability in students independent of linguistic, cultural, and socioeconomic background. Thus, the test is meant to be free from bias by eliminating elements of reading, writing, or speaking; instead, it utilizes abstract images, patterns, and designs. Scores from the NNAT are commonly used to place children in gifted and talented programs. The NNAT is ideal for English language learners or for students who are gifted but whose verbal reasoning or problem-solving skills are not ideal. The NNAT Level C tests students in second grade. This guide covers the sections on the NNAT3, specifically for Level C (Grade 2). In addition to information on each section, this guide offers practice questions and answers to help your student become familiar with the exam format and content.

Test Administration

The exam is offered twice a year in the Fall and early spring. The exam can be purchased through a Pearson specialist or through the Pearson website. Test administration is done locally, usually through your school district. Contact your school district to find out when they offer the test and what the procedure is within the classroom. Each school will have different rules regarding test administration.

Test Format

The exam is 30 minutes long with 48 multiple-choice questions and has both online and paper options. There are four sections in Level C: Pattern Completion, Reasoning by Analogy, Serial Reasoning, and Spatial Visualization.

Question Type	Description
Pattern Completion	Students must pick an answer choice that completes a missing part of the overall pattern.
Reasoning by Analogy	Students must find the relationship between two different images or sequences in order to find the missing square.
Serial Reasoning	Students must find a single missing square within a grid of shapes and sizes that represents an overall pattern.
Spatial Visualization	Students must decide which rotation the first row of boxes takes, then apply that rotation to the second row of boxes.

Scoring

The NNAT3 Online offers immediate reporting of scores once the test is complete, and home reports are available in Spanish and English. Score reports will consist of three different scores:

- Raw Score: This score is the number of items the student has answered correctly. If your student answered 35 questions correctly, the raw score will be "35/48."

- Naglieri Ability Index (NAI): The raw score will be converted using the NAI score, which compares your child to other children in the same age group who took the exam. Maximum scoring for this category is 160, and the average scoring for this category is 100.

- Percentile Rank: This score ranks your student among the national sample of students who take the NNAT. If your student comes home with a rank of 80%, that means that your student scored higher than 80% of students within the same age group.

Recent/Future Developments

The NNAT3 is the third edition of the NNAT with new developments, increased security, and a user-friendly online interface.

Pattern Completion

The Pattern Completion section is useful for Level C (second grade). Pattern Completion presents an overall design with one part of the design missing. Students are expected to find and choose the piece that completes the overall design. This section tests a student's ability to visually comprehend pattern analysis and its overall structure. A helpful tip to complete this section is to go through each answer choice and imagine the missing part inside the overall structure. If the choice completes the overall structure, then that will be the correct option to choose. Use the process of elimination to discard incorrect answers.

Relevance

How is pattern completion related to intelligence? Pattern completion deals with the part of the brain that makes inferences. Making an **inference** is when you are presented with only partial information and then rely on reasoning and evidence to determine the rest of the information. Completing patterns where only a partial amount of information is given helps the brain to "fill in" the information not shown. This type of neurological rehearsal is useful in almost every aspect of cognition. Additionally, social inferences, creative writing, and musical recognition are also related to visual pattern completion because the same "mechanism" in the brain is used to complete whatever pattern is in front of the student. Pattern completion is a critical tool for students in all aspects of their lives, and the practice of pattern completion will help exercise the part of the brain that relies on making inferences to solve problems.

Tips for Parents

For parents wanting to help their student with these problems, there are a few questions to ask the student before making a decision. While parent and student come in contact with the first question, point to the answer choices and ask the student, "which one of these, A, B, C, D, or E, do you think fits into this picture?" Then point to the large image where the section is missing. The student will then understand that he or she has to *fill in the blank*, so to speak, but with a patterned image. Parents can go down the choices one by one: "Does 'A' fit? Why or why not?" and so on until the correct answer is discovered. Complete three or four of the questions like this, and then back away and let the student finish the rest of the questions. Chances are, they will begin to silently ask themselves the same question you have been asking them. Check their answers afterward, and then go back over the ones they get incorrect.

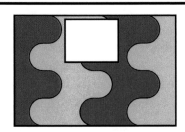
Sample Problems

Sample 1:

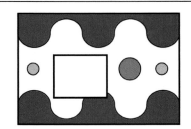

A   B   C   D   E

Sample 2:

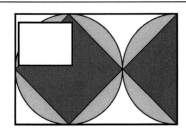

A   B   C   D   E

Sample 3:

A   B   C   D   E

Explanations of Sample Problems

1. C: Choice *C* is the best fit to complete this pattern. First let's look at the overall pattern. The colors are purple, yellow, purple, yellow, when looking from left to right. If we take the first yellow design and move it over the purple towards the second yellow design, the yellow areas will actually fit into each other neatly, as if they are parts of a puzzle piece. Now let's solve the question as if the two yellow sections were puzzle pieces. Would *A* complete the puzzle? No, because the box is all purple, and we need a yellow protrusion in order to fit at the top. Does *B* fit? No, because *B* has a purple protrusion, and we need a yellow protrusion. Does *C* fit? Yes, *C* has a yellow protrusion. If we placed "C" in the missing square, then the pattern would be complete. Additionally, if we imagined the two yellow pieces were puzzles, the image in *C* would fit perfectly into the piece.

2. B: Let's look at the way the circles coincide with the purple waves. When the purple protrudes, notice there is a yellow dot in the middle. When the purple recedes, notice there is an orange dot in the middle. The blank square is inserted in a place where the purple recedes then protrudes, going from left to right. Our circles must then coincide with "orange," "yellow," to match with the purple "receding" then "protruding." Choice *B* is the best answer here, because we have an orange then yellow circle from left to right. We also see the purple protrusion in the bottom right corner.

3. E: We can see that the overall pattern here is a maroon triangle inside of a yellow circle. Therefore, the bottom right of the box should include maroon, and the top left of the box should include a yellow strip. The only image that matches this description is Choice *E*. Pay attention to which way the edges of the triangle and circle are going. Choice *A* has the edges going the opposite direction of Choice *E*.

Reasoning by Analogy

The Reasoning by Analogy section is useful for Level C (second grade). Reasoning by Analogy prompts students to recognize relationships through the use of geometric shapes. In this section, there is a grid of squares, and each square contains shapes and shading. Students should look across the row or up and down the column to decide what the relationship is among the squares. One square will be empty. One technique is to visualize each answer choice in the empty square and decide if the relationship is consistent with the rest of the squares. This section requires students to comprehend both shapes and shading to visualize analogous relationships. The relationship in one row (or column) will have an analogous, or comparable, relationship in the next row (or column).

Relevance

How is Reasoning by Analogy related to intelligence? **Analogy** compares two objects or pairs of objects. It is the viewers' job to recognize the relationship between those objects. Analogical reasoning helps us understand relationships between things, but also asks us to *remember* relationships so that we can use the analogical reasoning for future comparisons. Analogical reasoning is necessary to human thought, and some consider analogical reasoning as a *basis* for human thought. Think of it like this: your student's teacher is trying to explain the concept of a "family tree." The students do not understand what the teacher is talking about. The teacher decides to use an analogy to explain. She gets out a single bunch of grapes and says: "These two grapes at the top are a mom and dad. The five grapes coming from the mom and dad grapes are their children. The grapes along this stem horizontal from the mom and dad are the mom's siblings," and so on. The concept clicks in the student's minds, because the teacher has used an analogy. She has shown that a similar relationship exists within another space, and since the students understand this primary relationship, they can apply it to the new relationship. Learning could very well stem from analogy to analogy—it is a way for humans to understand concepts within the world.

Tips for Parents

For parents to help their students with these problems, you can ask your student a question before they do each of the problems. Have the problem in front of you. The top row will be complete, and a relationship will exist within the top row. Say, "Look at the top row. Each of the squares has a relationship with the other in some way. Now look at the bottom row. Can you find a square that completes the bottom row in the same way as the top row?" The student will pick a square that completes the relationship. Do this for about four or five problems, then let the student proceed on their own. They will silently start to ask themselves about the relationships between the rows.

Sample Problems

Sample 1:

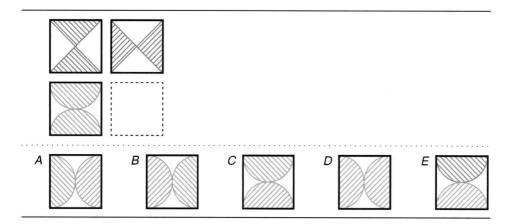

Sample 2:

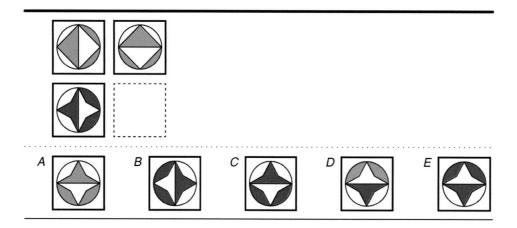

Sample 3:

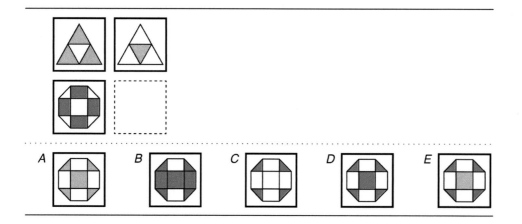

Explanations of Sample Problems

1. D: Because these are analogical relationships, we should look at the first row and decide what's going on. The picture starts out as a shape like an hourglass on the left. The picture to the right looks like an hourglass turned on its side. So, what's happening with the relationship between the two top squares? If we flip the first square on its side, it becomes the second image! Let's do the same with the two squares below. We have a sort of rounded hourglass figure on the bottom left square that looks like two bubbles placed together. We want to turn this square on its side so that we match the relationship between the two top squares. But that's not all. We see that Choices *A*, *B*, and *D* are all turned on their side. When we look at the stripes inside the first two squares, we can see that the stripes are the same from when the square is upright to when it's on its side. Let's pick the same stripes inside the bottom figures as well. In the bottom left figure, the stripes are both angling toward the left. Choice *A* is incorrect, because in the bottom bubble, the stripes are angling toward the right. Choice *B* is incorrect, because in the top bubble, the stripes are angling toward the right. Choice *D* is the best answer because both set of stripes are angling toward the left, just like in the original image on bottom.

2. C: Sample 2 is similar to Sample 1. The top two squares have a relationship with each other, and we have to figure out their relationship before we move on. If you take the square at the top left and turn it clockwise, we get the figure on the right. Therefore, the bottom left image must be turned clockwise in order to find the bottom right image. What image do we get when we turn the bottom left clockwise? We get Choice *C*. Choice *E* is close because it has the same shapes. However, the shading is incorrect in Choice *E*, because the top would be white and the bottom would be purple, and the opposite is true. Choice *C* is the exact image of the bottom left image turned clockwise, so this is our best answer.

3. D: Sample 3 is tricky. The relationship between the top squares is that everything is transposed. The top left shows us a white triangle inside of a yellow triangle. The top right shows us a yellow triangle inside of a white triangle. Now let's look at the bottom left image. There are orange rectangles inside of a white circle. We know that a comparable relationship would be transposing this image. So, let's look for white rectangles inside of an orange circle. This would be Choice *D*, which has white rectangles inside of an orange circle. The colors are perfectly transposed from left box to right box.

Serial Reasoning

The Serial Reasoning is useful for Level C test takers (second grade). In Serial Reasoning, students are presented with a grid of nine, three-by-three boxes. Each box contains a shape, color, and/or rotation, and the boxes will display an overall design. When students trace their fingers down the rows or columns, a serial pattern can be recognized. Each question displays an empty box, and the students must figure out which shape belongs in that box.

Studying Reading by Analogy questions will help students master the Serial Reasoning questions because the presentation of the question is similar. However, the two have their differences. Reasoning by Analogy relies on the understanding of analogy, or comparison, to answer the question. In Reasoning by Analogy, a student may ask, "How does the top row compare to the bottom row, and how can I use this information to find the blank box?" In Serial Reasoning, the students' ability to recognize an overall pattern is again tested, but this time in a grid sequence rather than an already-developed shape like Pattern Completion. Essentially, Serial Reasoning tests students' abilities to find the missing element within a matrix of geometric shapes.

Relevance

How is serial reasoning related to intelligence? Serial reasoning, in this exam, is used with shapes and sizes. But serial reasoning also exists within language and the thought process that goes with language. Serial reasoning within language is when you begin with one statement, which supports a second statement, which supports a third statement. Kind of like this:

> I'm staying inside because it's so cold outside, so you have to stay inside too.

> Statement 1: I'm staying inside

> (Supports) Statement 2: Because it's so cold outside

> (Supports) Statement 3: So you have to stay inside too.

Patterns of reasoning are also used in serial reasoning. You are given a single square. The next two squares relate to the first square in some way. They are either bigger or smaller. They are either shaded or not shaded. Students must look for this pattern of reasoning within one line and relate it to the pattern as a whole. Just like in the language above—students see that the pattern of statements lends to an argument as a whole, which is a persuasive argument to stay indoors. The one square that is missing can be backtracked by looking at the boxes that align with it and seeing how it fits within the whole image.

Tips for Parents

For parents to help their students with these problems, you can ask your student a question before they do each of the problems. Have the problem in front of you. Say, "There is a row across. See how the shape changes? Now look at the row down. See how the shape changes?" It may help to say the changes out loud, like "Big, Small, Big," to find the pattern. Then when the child gets to the missing square, they may be able to find the missing piece with the word pattern. Do four or five of these with your student, asking them the same question. Then, let them do the rest alone. They should be asking

themselves the same question, moving across and down the image to find the pattern, and ultimately finding the missing square.

Sample Problems

Sample 1:

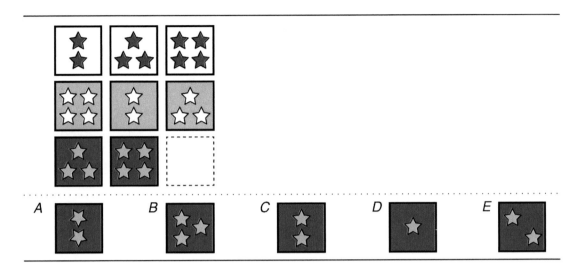

Sample 2:

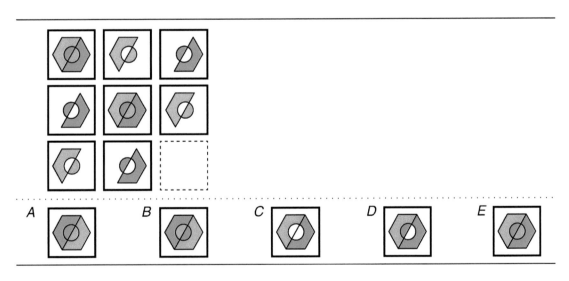

Explanations of Sample Problems

1. C: Let's look at the top row first. We see that each square in the top row has a box with 2 stars, 3 stars, and then 4 stars. The same is true of the second row. We see a box with 2 stars, 3 stars, and 4 stars. Now let's look at the bottom row. We see a box with 3 stars and 4 stars, but we see no box with 2 stars. We know that we need a 2-star box, so our answer will be either Choice *A, C*, or *E*. What do the other 2-star boxes look like in the matrix? Both of them have stars in a vertical alignment, which leaves us Choices *A* and *C*. In the original boxes, we can see that the 2 vertically-aligned stars have points that are facing straight up on each of the stars. Does Choice *A* have points facing straight up? No, in Choice *A* the stars' points are facing down. In Choice *C*, we see that the stars' points are facing straight up. Therefore, Choice *C* is the best answer.

2. E: In this problem, we see the same shapes in every row. In the top row, there is a yellow half, green half, then an image where the two halves are placed together. The same goes for the second row. We also see the same if we looked at the images as columns. Each column has a yellow half, green half, then a whole comprised of those two halves. In the third row we are missing the whole, or the two halves put together. We have two halves put together in all answer choices, so we have to look and see what the other images look like. The green and yellow figures in the matrix have yellow on the top left, green on the bottom right, green half circle on top left, and a yellow half circle on bottom right. The only image that fits this description is Choice *E*, so this is the best answer.

Spatial Visualization

General Overview

The Spatial Visualization is used by Level C test takers (second grade). In Spatial Visualization, test takers are shown a matrix of four separate boxes. The first row will contain two boxes with the same two-dimensional shapes inside. However, the only difference between the shapes is that they are rotated in different directions. The second row will contain two boxes as well. The first box in the second row will contain a shape or set of shapes, like the first, but the second box in the second row will be empty. Students must decide which rotation belongs in the blank box by mirroring which rotation was used for the first row of boxes.

Spatial visualization is the capability of visually manipulating a two-dimensional shape in order to match it analogically to a set of boxes beside it. Students must first decide which way the set of shapes were rotated, and then students must use analogy to apply the same rotation to the second row. The greatest difficulty of Spatial Visualization is that some of the incorrect answer choices will swap color, shape, as well as rotation in order to trick the test taker into choosing an incorrect choice. Therefore, students must make sure the colors and shapes of their chosen rotation matches the colors and shapes in the original square.

Relevance

How is spatial visualization related to intelligence and what is its relevance? Spatial visualization shows an individual's ability to manipulate objects to suit a specific purpose. Building Legos, using a map, or organizing blocks are activities that are related to spatial intelligence. Professions that rely on spatial visualization skills include engineers, artists, graphic designers, surgeons, photographers, geologists, and architects.

Tips for Parents

For parents attempting to help their student with these problems, sit down with your student and ask them about the matrix. Say, "See the first row? There are two boxes that have the same image, but the image is rotated. What kind of rotation does the image make from left to right?" If the image that faced up is now facing to the right, you can say, "the image turned from facing upward toward the right." Then go to the second row to the blank box and say, "now we have to find the image below that moves to face the right side." Let you student study the images below for a few moments before helping them. It may take time. They can mark out which images do not turn toward the right, then eliminate the images that change color or shape. Process of elimination might work best for these questions.

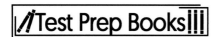

Sample Problems

Sample 1:

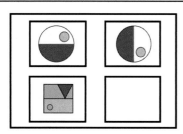

A   B   C   D   E

Sample 2:

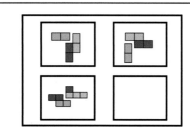

A   B   C   D   E

Sample 3:

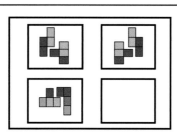

A   B   C   D   E

Explanations of Sample Problems

1. D: Let's look at the top row first. The box on the left contains a circle. Half of the circle is colored purple, with a small yellow circle inside. The box on the right shows the same set of shapes, except the box is turned on its right side. Now let's apply the right-facing rotation to the second row of boxes. The shape in the second row is a square with blue on top, yellow on bottom, a blue circle in the yellow area, and a purple triangle facing downward in the blue area. Now, in our minds, we turn the second-row box on its right side. The correct answer is Choice *D*. If we turned our heads to the right, we would notice that the set of shapes are exactly the same, only flipped on its right side.

2. C: In this problem, we see that the first box in the first row contains a blue, green, and red figure made up of two blocks. In the second box of the first row, the figure appears to have turned on its left side, because we see that the blue figure is now on the left side rather than at the top of the box. Now, let's apply the same left-facing rotation to the second row. In the second row, we see that at the top there is a red block, then yellow blocks, then purple blocks, then blue blocks. Choice *C* is the best answer because if we flipped the image on its left side, it would match up completely. Choice *B* is close; the red block is at the top as it is in Choice *C*. However, we know from the original image that the yellow blocks stick out toward the red block's right side, and in Choice *B*, the yellow blocks stick out toward the red block's left side (when looking at the image sideways). Choice *C* is the correct answer here.

3. B: This problem is more difficult because the image in the first row, first box, is rotated clockwise (or to the right) two times. Basically, it is a mirror image from the first box to the second box. Let's use the mirror analogy to solve this problem. If the second row image was mirrored, we would have at the very right of the image a single blue box. We see that both Choices *C* and *B* have this characteristic. However, we also can see that if we mirrored the original box, the stack of three boxes that are blue, orange, and red, would be imitated in Choice *B*, while Choice *C* has the three boxes opposite of the correct answer.

Pattern Completion

1

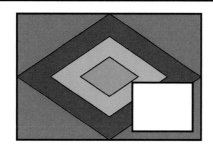

A   B   C   D   E

2

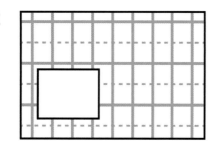

A   B   C   D   E

3

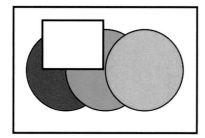

A   B   C   D   E

4

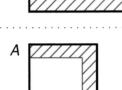

A 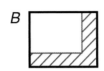   B    C    D 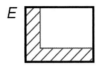   E

5

A    B    C    D    E

6

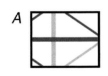

A 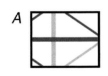   B    C 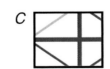   D 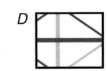   E

7

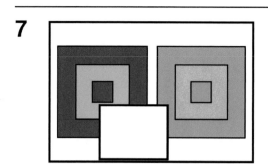

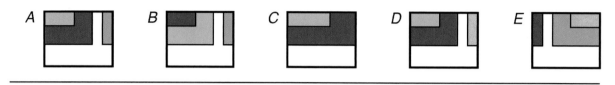

8

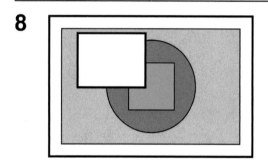

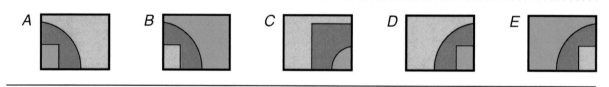

9

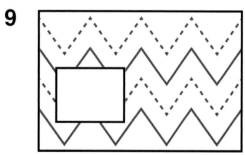

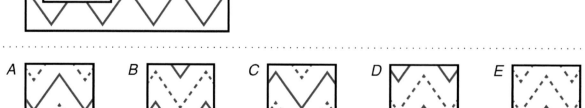

10

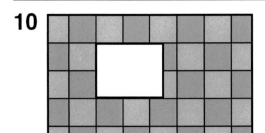

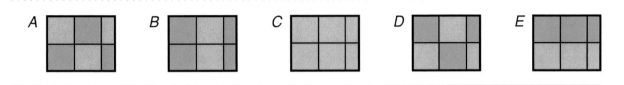

11

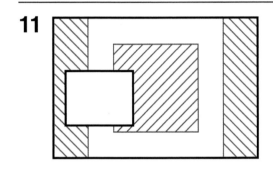

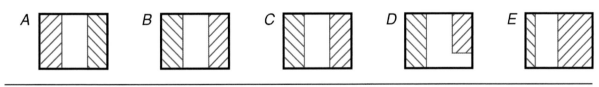

12

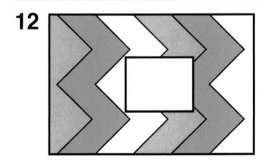

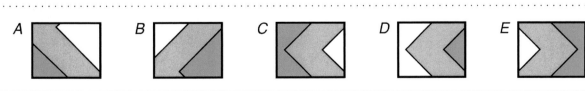

Reasoning by Analogy

1

A   B   C   D   E

2

A   B   C   D   E

3

A   B   C   D   E

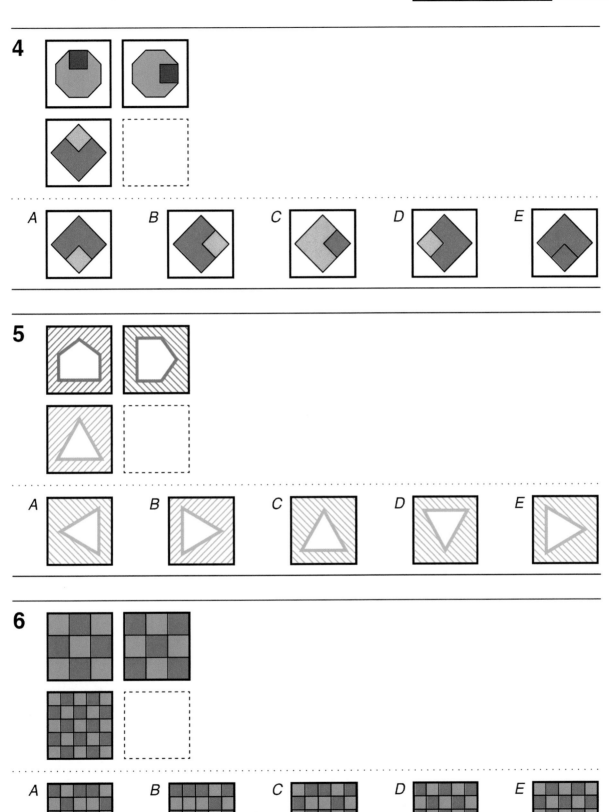

7

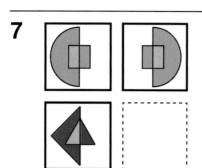

A 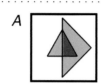   B   C   D   E

8

A 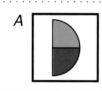   B   C   D   E

9

A 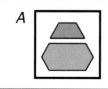   B   C 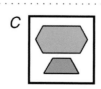   D 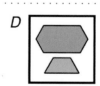   E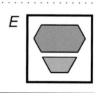

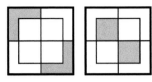

10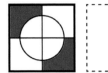

A   B   C   D   E

11

A   B   C   D   E

12

A   B   C   D   E

Serial Reasoning

1

A B C D E

2

A B C D E

3

A B C D E

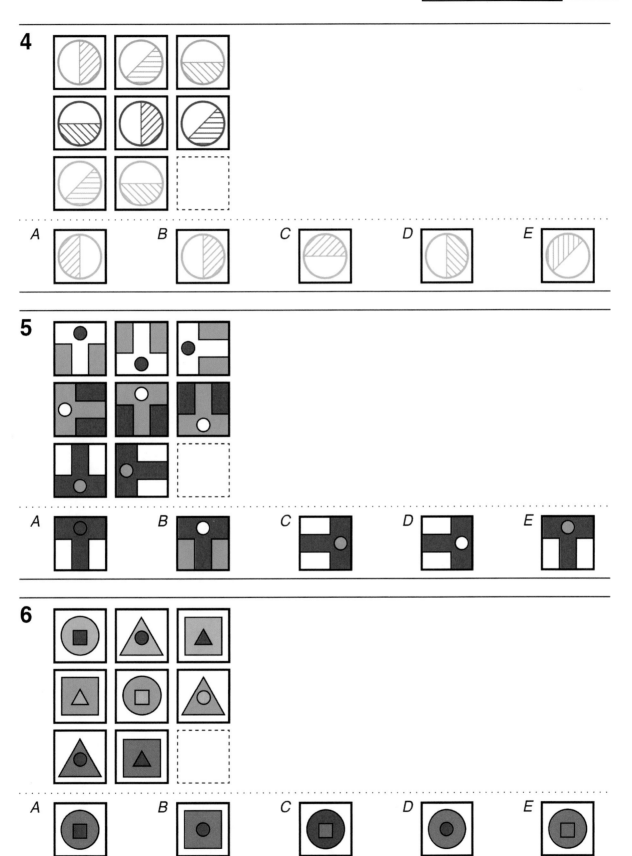

7

A 　　B 　　C 　　D 　　E

8

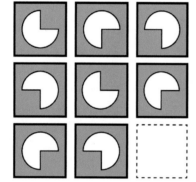

A 　　B 　　C 　　D 　　E

9

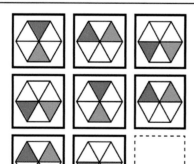

A 　　B 　　C 　　D 　　E

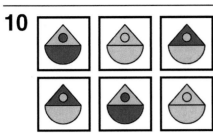

10

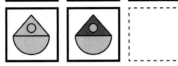

 A   B   C   D   E

11

A B   C   D   E

A   B   C   D   E

12

Spatial Visualization

1

A B C D E

2

A B C D E

3

A B C D E

4

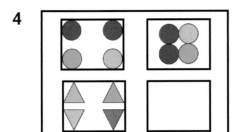

A   B   C   D   E

5

A   B   C   D   E

6

A B   C   D   E

7

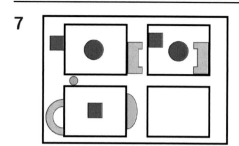

 A   B   C   D   E

8

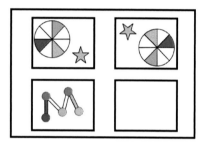

 A   B   C   D   E

9

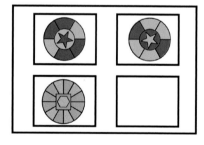

A B C D E

10 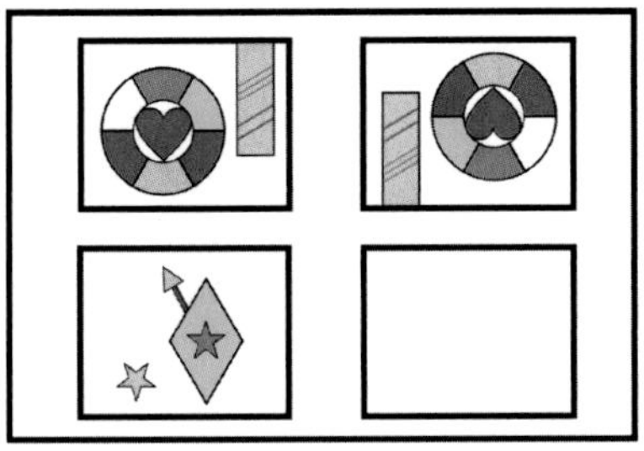

A 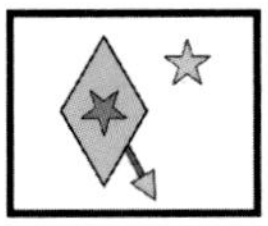 B 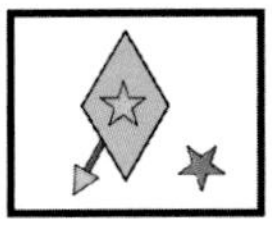 C 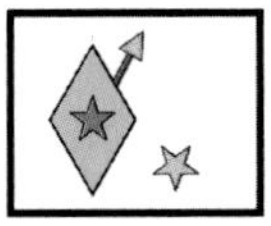 D 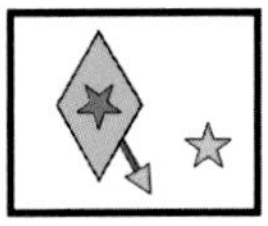 E 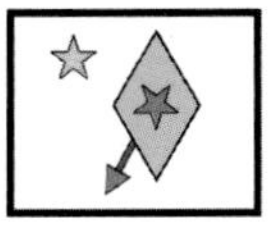

11 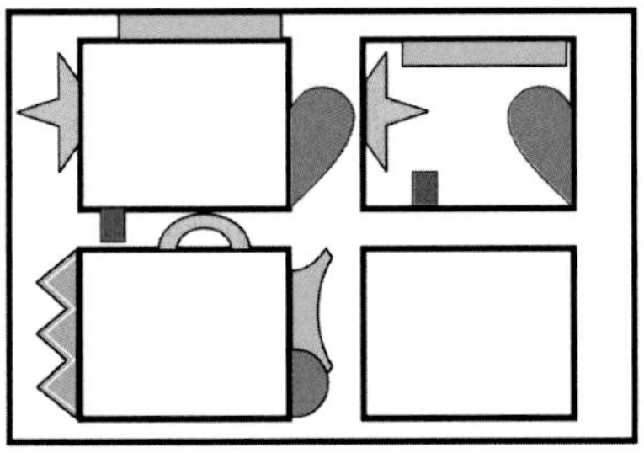

A 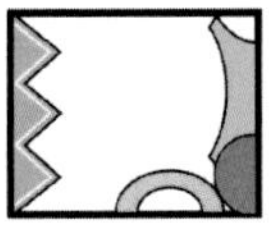 B 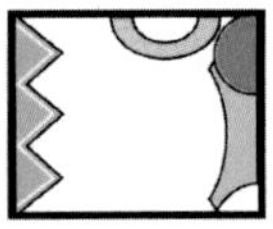 C 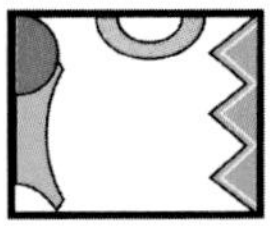 D 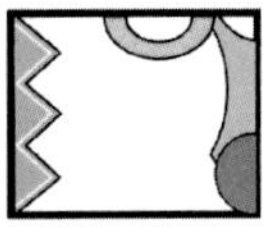 E 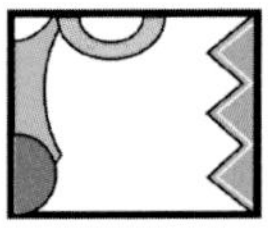

12 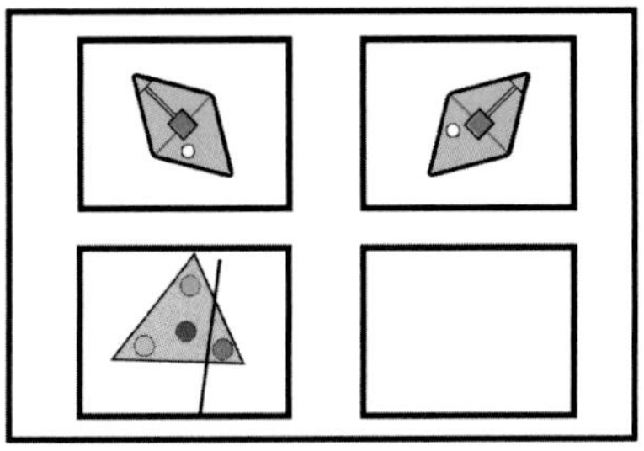

A 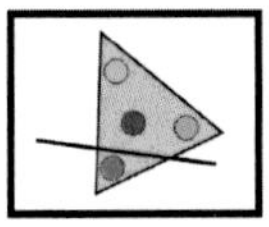 B 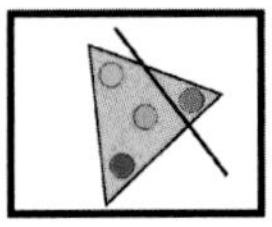 C 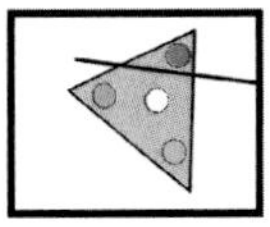 D 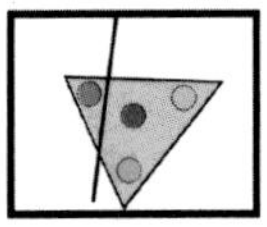 E 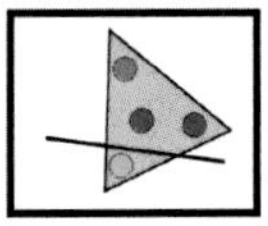

Answer Explanations #1

Answers

Pattern Completion

1: C	2: E	3: D	4: A	5: C	6: E

7: A	8: D	9: D	10: D	11: B	12: D

Reasoning by Analogy

1: E	2: C	3: A	4: B	5: E	6: D

7: B	8: A	9: D	10: B	11: C	12: E

Serial Reasoning

1: A	2: B	3: C	4: B	5: E	6: A

7: D	8: C	9: C	10: E	11: B	12: C

Spatial Visualization

1: D	2: E	3: A	4: B	5: A	6: E

7: B	8: C	9: A	10: A	11: D	12: A

Pattern Completion

1

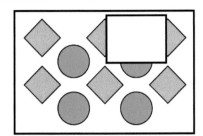

A   B   C   D   E

2

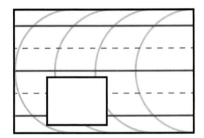

A   B   C   D   E

3

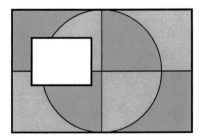

A   B   C   D   E

4

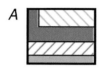 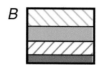 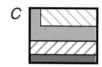 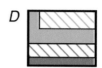

A B C D E

5

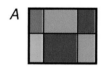 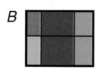 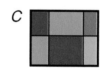

A B C D E

6

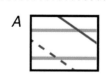 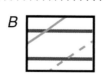 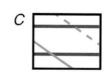 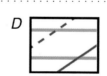 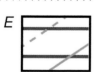

A B C D E

7

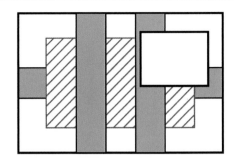

A   B   C   D   E

8

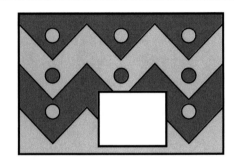

A   B   C   D   E

9

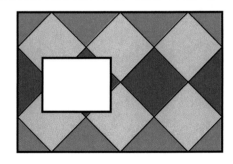

A   B   C   D   E

10

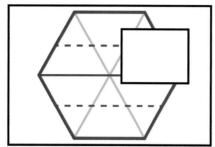

A B C D E

11

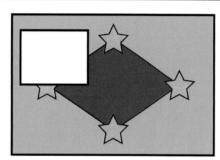

A B C D E

12

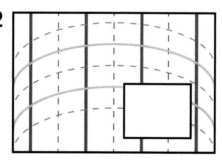

A B C D E

Reasoning by Analogy

1

A   B   C   D   E

2

A   B   C   D   E

3

A   B   C   D   E

4

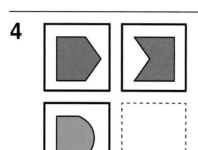

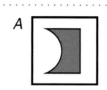

A   B   C   D   E

5

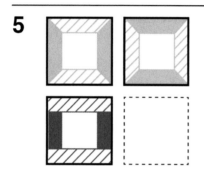

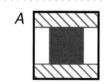

A   B   C   D   E

6

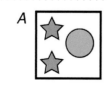   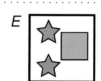

A   B   C   D   E

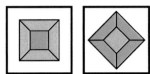

7

A   B   C   D   E

8

A   B   C   D   E

9

A   B   C   D   E

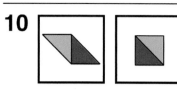
10

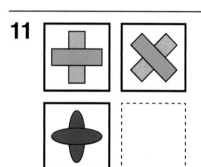

A 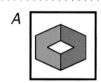   B   C   D   E

11

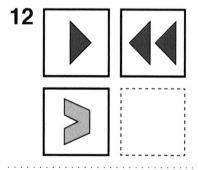

A 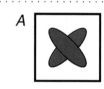   B   C   D 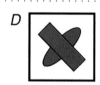   E

12

A 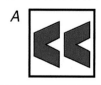   B   C   D   E

Serial Reasoning

1

2

3

4

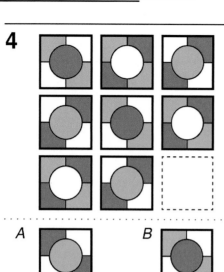

A   B   C   D   E

5

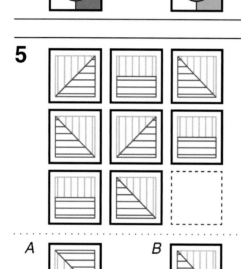

A   B   C   D   E

6

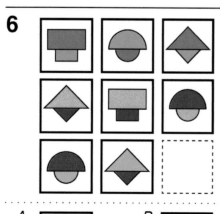

A   B   C   D   E

7

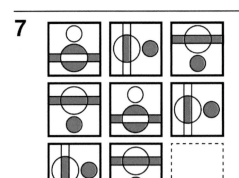

A
B
C
D
E

8

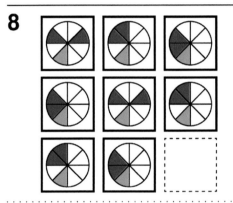

A
B
C
D
E

9

A
B
C
D
E

10

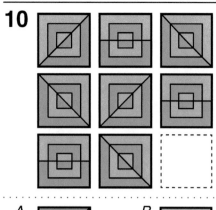

A   B   C   D   E

11

A   B   C   D   E

12

A   B   C   D   E

Spatial Visualization

1

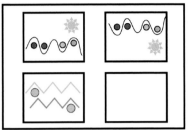

A   B   C   D   E

2

A   B   C   D   E

3

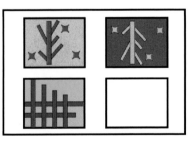

A   B   C   D   E

4

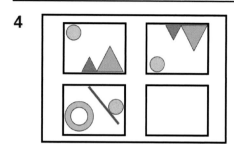

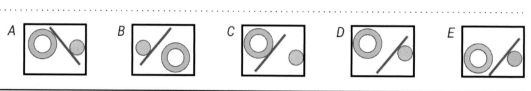

5

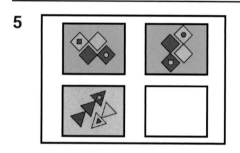

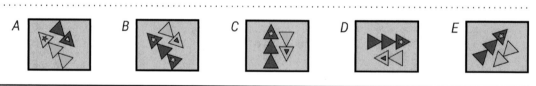

6

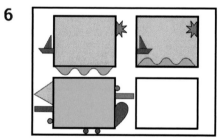

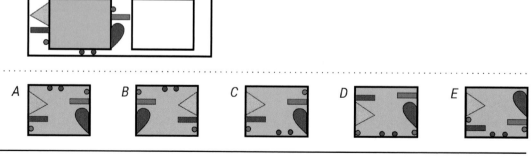

7

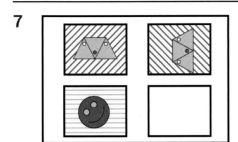

A   B   C   D   E

8

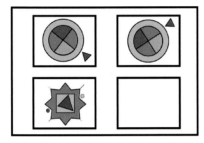

A   B   C   D   E

9

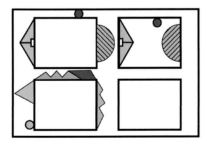

A   B   C   D  E

10

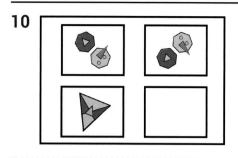

A   B   C   D   E

11

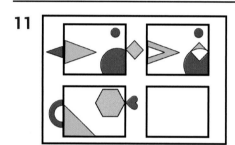

A   B   C   D   E

12

A   B   C   D   E

Answer Explanations #2

Answers

Pattern Completion

1: D	2: B	3: D	4: C	5: A	6: E

7: A	8: D	9: B	10: A	11: E	12: C

Reasoning by Analogy

1: A	2: C	3: D	4: B	5: C	6: E

7: A	8: D	9: D	10: C	11: A	12: B

Serial Reasoning

1: B	2: D	3: E	4: B	5: C	6: A

7: D	8: C	9: B	10: E	11: B	12: E

Spatial Visualization

1: C	2: D	3: B	4: D	5: A	6: C

7: B	8: E	9: A	10: C	11: B	12: D

FREE Test Taking Tips DVD Offer

To help us better serve you, we have developed a Test Taking Tips DVD that we would like to give you for FREE. **This DVD covers world-class test taking tips that you can use to be even more successful when you are taking your test.**

All that we ask is that you email us your feedback about your study guide. Please let us know what you thought about it – whether that is good, bad or indifferent.

To get your **FREE Test Taking Tips DVD**, email freedvd@studyguideteam.com with "FREE DVD" in the subject line and the following information in the body of the email:

    a. The title of your study guide.

    b. Your product rating on a scale of 1-5, with 5 being the highest rating.

    c. Your feedback about the study guide. What did you think of it?

    d. Your full name and shipping address to send your free DVD.

If you have any questions or concerns, please don't hesitate to contact us at freedvd@studyguideteam.com.

Thanks again!